Recruiting
Volunteers

Abingdon Press & The Church of the Resurrection
Ministry Guides

Recruiting
Volunteers

Dan Entwistle
Adam Hamilton, Series Editor

ABINGDON PRESS
Nashville

RECRUITING VOLUNTEERS

Copyright © 2007 by Abingdon Press

This book is printed on acid-free paper.

Library of Congress Cataloging-in-Publication Data

Entwistle, Dan.
  Recruiting volunteers / Dan Entwistle.
      p. cm. – (Abingdon Press & the Church of the Resurrection ministry guides ; 4)
    ISBN-13: 978-0-687-46641-2 (pbk. : alk. paper)
   1. Voluntarism–Religious aspects–Christianity. I. Title.
   BR115.V64E58 2007
   253'.7–dc22

                                                                          2007016830

07 08 09 10 11 12 13 14 15 16—10 9 8 7 6 5 4 3 2 1
MANUFACTURED IN THE UNITED STATES OF AMERICA

Contents

Foreword

God created each of us with an inherent desire to make a difference. As Christians, we've been gifted and empowered by the Holy Spirit for service. We were ordained in our baptism and confirmation to ministry for Christ. Hence, as church leaders, we are not simply about recruiting volunteers, but helping people fulfill God's call on their lives, growing as Christ's disciples, and finding fulfillment and joy through ministry. As we help people do this, the work of the ministry of the church multiplies exponentially.

The fact that you've purchased this guide indicates that you know already your church will never reach its full potential unless you become adept at inviting your laity to do the work of the ministry. Dan Entwistle has, nearly from our church's inception, been an important part of recruiting, training, and deploying our laypeople in ministry. He knows that the goal is not simply to "get the job done," but to help those who are volunteering to grow as disciples of Jesus Christ and to experience the joy of serving. In this guide, he shares with you some of the things we've learned about inviting persons to be in ministry through the church.

In developing these guides, we listened to the requests of smaller churches for practical resources to help in strengthening their churches. Few things are more important to this than recruiting volunteers.

· ·

At The Church of the Resurrection, we live daily with the goal to help people become deeply committed Christians. More than nominally religious. More than the Sunday pew holder. More than the spectator. We know these same people become more by doing more. We begin with the knowledge that people want the church to be theirs. They want to know God has a place for them. With that in mind, we recognized from the very start that specialized ministries utilizing the skills and talents of laypeople are fundamental to church life.

A church on the move will have specialized ministries capitalizing on the skills and talents of laypeople. They are your keys to succeed.

In developing these guides, we listened to the requests of smaller churches for practical resources to enlist laypeople for this purpose. These economical guides, written by proven leaders at our church, will serve as essential resources for innovative, creative, and, more than likely, nontraditional church workers who have little or no budget to work with. With these guides in hand, your laypeople will be ready to plunge into the work with excitement and courage instead of tentatively approaching it on tiptoe.

At the core of these guides is the belief that anything is possible. It's a challenge, but it's a truth. God can and does use us all—with that conviction we bring hope to the world.

Adam Hamilton
Senior Pastor
The Church of the Resurrection
Leawood, Kansas

CHAPTER ONE

Addressing the Pinch Point

Whether you attend a church of ten people or ten thousand, God has provided you with a valuable resource that is untapped. She sits in the pew next to you every week. He joined the church last year. They just entered into their retirement years. She was just confirmed and is eager to apply what she learned. They each yearn, whether they know it or not, to become involved, to give back, to make their lives count. God created them for this—to spend their time, to give their lives—for something bigger than themselves, something that will make an eternal difference. While your church already has volunteers (you may even be one of them), you picked up this ministry guide because you are ready to see your church become more effective.

Whether you are a staff member, lay leader, or a faithful volunteer, you have a mandate to equip the people of the church for ministry (Eph. 4:11-13). Not because the church must fill volunteer positions, but because on its best day the church is a movement of people following God into an adventure of ministry. And, enrolling Christians in the mission of the church is imperative.

A Pass-Fail Challenge

A few years back, I was in a meeting to discuss volunteerism in my church. We were struggling and we knew it. We lamented about a lack of volunteers across several of our church's key ministries. As a church with thousands in attendance every weekend, and well over half our members volunteering, we still couldn't seem to adequately resource our ministry dreams. So, as leaders in the church, we knew this was a pass-fail challenge—one that we had to address. I stepped to the whiteboard and drew a picture resembling an hourglass turned on its side. On the left side of the hourglass I wrote "The potential." On the right, "The resources."

PINCH POINT

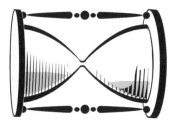

THE POTENTIAL

THE RESOURCES

A closer look

 ⇨ **The potential:** God desires to do something through your church that is far from mundane. You are engaged in the mission of God—full of surprises and wonderment.

- In children's ministry, you aren't babysitting. You have an opportunity to shape the lives of children, teaching them to pray for the first time, providing safety and trust in an unsure world, shaping their lives with hope and grace, and helping young ones discover God's mission for their lives.

- In evangelism, you aren't making members. You are introducing lost people to the One in whom they will be found, offering hope to hurting folks, and introducing them to a life that really matters.
- In music ministry, you aren't performing for the audience. You are leading God's people in heartfelt worship, helping them experience the gospel in ways words alone cannot, and providing a foretaste of heaven.

God has bigger dreams for our ministry than we can see; our mission isn't completely fulfilled yet. The church isn't too big to accept your friend's sister who is a spiritual seeker. Your missions ministry hasn't entirely undone the ills of poverty in your community. Your ministry with teenagers hasn't yet shaped the life of every high school student in your community who is eager to discover what God has prepared for his or her life. What will it take for us to press into this future?

Resources

▷ **The resources:** On the right-hand side of the hourglass are the resources. Ministry dreams will be realized with God's greatest ministry resource, people. This is how it has always worked. Consider Abraham, Moses, Mary, Peter, and Paul. Scripture is chock-full of seemingly ordinary people empowered to do extraordinary things—world changers each with their own mixture of self-doubt and confidence. People who, perhaps, could have done a hundred other things but instead were found worthy of participating in God's work. They were inspired by a vision and empowered by the Spirit. Your congregation has people too. They, too, can make the difference. Sure, the potential is vast and the resources are within reach. But there is a pinch point in your church, just like mine.

▷ **The pinch point:** There are limits. In the narrow section of the hourglass we find ourselves restricted, just like a garden hose turned on high with a kink in the middle. This is the pinch we aim to address in this guidebook. We desire to unleash the potential of our churches: a ministry with healthy *volunteer practices* holds greater potential for success. We are called to stretch wide the narrow part of the hourglass, to unkink the hose. And if we succeed, ministry has the potential to flourish like never before. What is called for are people who are *invited* into ministry, *connected* to a significant role, *equipped* for service, and *sustained* in their efforts. So, in the following chapters, let's take a look at each of the four key components of volunteer management: *invite, connect, equip,* and *sustain.*

Invite

Time is precious. Our fellow church members know this. Time management experts advise us to be careful about the commitments we make with our time. We should budget our time in order to fulfill our highest priorities. Basic Time Management 101, right? So we divide our time judiciously between family, work, sleep, solitude, and recreation. Is it any wonder we have little time to take on additional commitments? Unlike other resources, we simply cannot create more time; it is a limited resource. Potential volunteers have 31,557,600 seconds to divide between all of their priorities this year. How will they decide to spend them?

Have you ever attended a wedding when you weren't invited or celebrated at a birthday party for a child you didn't know? I surely hope not! Truth is, we respond to invitations.

My family shared a spaghetti dinner with friends last week. We showed up at their house in response to a warm personal invitation. After hours of great conversation, we returned to our home. We had a great time of fellowship because we were invited. It wouldn't have been enough for them to clean their house and prepare dinner. The invitation had to be extended. "Build it and they will come" is a great line in a movie, but it makes for a flimsy model of volunteer ministry.

Strategy of Invitation

A well-developed strategy of invitation has three key aspects: (1) assessing volunteer opportunities, (2) creating entry points, and (3) spreading the word.

1. Assessing volunteer opportunities

Job one is to become an expert at "employee" acquisition, training, and development—just as with any business. While the success of a business hinges on the ability to hire and keep a great staff, the stakes are even higher in the church because our goal is far beyond profitability. We are aiming to see lives and communities transformed by the gospel. No matter what area of ministry you are leading, your success will depend on the team of volunteers you bring along. Begin developing your staffing plan by completing a Staffing Needs Analysis.

Staffing needs analysis

Before inviting others, you need a clearheaded idea of the ministry opportunities available. How many volunteers do you need? How many would you like to have? How many volunteers would it take to make the ministry soar? The majority of churches have two or fewer staff members, and in thousands of churches even the preacher is a volunteer. No matter how many staff members serve at your church, God's plan includes volunteers. Effectiveness for the ministry as a whole will rise and fall on the ministry of your church's volunteers.

 ▷ **List** the roles. To assess the number of potential volunteer roles in your ministry, conduct a Staffing Needs Analysis. At a planning meeting, tape chart paper to the wall and create a chart like the one found on page 16. On the chart, break your program area into all the possible roles where volunteers can serve.

Note: If you don't already have a list of volunteer roles, you may want to begin by creating sticky notes. Each note should list a distinct activity that must occur in order for the ministry to be fully supported. These notes can be sorted and categorized into volunteer positions until you have developed a list of various roles in your area. If your ministry area has a staff member, include key elements of that work. Chances are, there are pieces of the job that could be capably handled by a volunteer. In some circumstances, volunteers may bring more time, greater energy, or perhaps a certain expertise to the task. Offloading or delegating responsibilities from a staff member is good stewardship and a great way to expand your ministry without increasing your budget.

▷ **Quantify** the opportunities. Carefully consider how many volunteers it would take for the ministry to Survive, Maintain, and Thrive.

- **Survive.** This is the number of people required for you to open the doors and safely meet the needs of the current participants in your program. At this number there is no cushion, no room for growth. You're vulnerable. If you stay in survival mode for very long, you can expect your program to suffer and decline.

- **Maintain.** This would allow the volunteers to have a reasonable workload. At this level, participation in your program might remain steady or perhaps increase or decrease incrementally. Volunteers are fully engaged, but they're only able to cover the basics.

- **Thrive.** This is your program's sweet spot. Here, you're able to be innovative, taking on new ideas and challenges. Volunteers still feel the challenge of ministry, but they are refreshed and confident. They know they are part of a growing ministry that is humming along on all cylinders.

STEP 1: NEEDS ANALYSIS CHART (example)

POSITION	SURVIVE	MAINTAIN	THRIVE
Sunday School Greeters	1	3	5
Sixth Grade SS Teacher	2	4	8
Youth Retreat Adult Sponsors	4	6	8
Youth Newsletter Writer/Editor	1	1	2
TOTAL	**8**	**14**	**23**

▷ **Create** a Variance Chart. (See page 17.) Here's where you'll begin to gain a clearer picture of volunteer needs. Start by listing each of the positions. Then fill in the first column with the number of volunteers you currently have serving for each position. Finally, fill out the remainder of the chart with the variances by subtracting the number of volunteers needed (from the Needs Analysis Chart) from the current number of volunteers. You may want to list the negative numbers in red.

STEP 2: VARIANCE CHART (example)

POSITION	CURRENT VOLUNTEERS	SURVIVE VARIANCE	MAINTAIN VARIANCE	THRIVE VARIANCE
Sunday School Greeters	2	1	-1	-3
6th Grade SS Teacher	2	0	-2	-6
Youth Retreat Adult Sponsors	5	1	-1	-3
Youth Newsletter Writer/Editor	1	0	0	-1
TOTAL	**10**	**2**	**-4**	**-13**

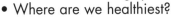

⇨ **Reflect.** With your team, take a look at the chart and ask the following questions:
- Where are we healthiest?
- Where are we poised to thrive?
- Where is our program currently vulnerable?
- Are there areas with a critical volunteer shortage?
- Do we have any surpluses? If so, should we consider reallocating volunteers to other areas of greater need?
- For our program to become more effective, how many new volunteers might we need to add?

Now that you are aware of the volunteer opportunities, be prepared to share this information with anyone who will listen. Let's say someone compliments your program. This is a golden opportunity. This person is catching your vision for ministry. Be prepared to take the conversation to the next level. You might want to say something simple, like this: "Thank you for your encouraging words—I absolutely love doing this. And you know, we're always growing and changing. I'd love to tell you more. In fact, is there any chance we can catch coffee together this week to talk?"

Big, audacious ideas

In addition to current openings, you may want to keep a separate list of new ministry ideas—ambitious, extraordinary ideas for which you sense God's "yes" for your church. Take care to make sure the ideas are true to your church's purpose and vision, but allow God to stretch your thinking into new, innovative areas. Keep the list at your desk or inside your Bible. Armed with this list, begin to pray for the leadership to emerge. You may even discover that someone in your church (maybe even a current volunteer) has been waiting in the wings ready for just such a challenge. So, keep your eyes wide open to see if God brings someone across your path.

Staying ahead

Is your church short on paid staff? Is the budget so tight that even basic positions remain understaffed? You're not alone. This is true of churches of all sizes. It doesn't seem to matter whether the church is growing or shrinking. (In growing churches the ministry demands outpace available staffing dollars and in shrinking churches funds tend to be directed toward keeping the building open and operational.) At The Church of the Resurrection, our ministry leaders will tell you we are chronically understaffed. There just never seems to be enough money in the budget to stay ahead of the staffing needs.

But I have good news. The secret is, there are relatively few tasks that actually require a paid staff member. Furthermore, one of the worst mistakes a church can make is to hire professionals to do the work of the people of the church. Of course, when the ministry takes on a certain size, staff members become essential. But the primary responsibility of staff, both lay and clergy, is to equip the people of the church for ministry. The church belongs first to God and secondly to the people. Professional staff members should wake up in the morning looking for a more effective way to facilitate the ministry of the congregation. They'll lead the way, but they do so primarily by inviting, connecting, equipping, and sustaining volunteers.

At The Church of the Resurrection, we take this issue seriously. In fact, staff members are formally evaluated during their annual reviews with respect to how well they contributed to the ministry of volunteers. High-performing go-it-alone professionals find that a solo-leadership style is out of place in the church.

Years ago I was challenged by a veteran leader in my field of ministry. He asked, "If you were to receive a list today containing the names of twenty additional people eager to serve in your ministry, where would you most need them?" Fact is, most of us aren't prepared to answer that question. Too often, we construct our ministries around surviving. I find that we often scale back our dreams to match our current situation. As ministry leaders, we should dream big, pray hard, and always stand prepared to deploy people into Christian service.

2. Creating entry points

Many of us grew up in the church, but an increasing number of spiritual seekers without church experience are showing up with high hopes of important, world-changing work to be done in the church. They need an entry point, a safe place to get started. They bring questions along with them: "Will I find joy in the service?" "Will I be appropriately challenged?" "Do I care about the ministry vision enough to give it more of my time?"

An idea from one church is to provide visitors and new members with a list of "Good Start" options. The list allows new people to know they can find a great place to get started. And ministry leaders know they are expected to offer entry-level ministry experiences that are tailored to the newcomer. This "tiering" of volunteer roles is one of the best ways your church can contribute to the development of a new volunteer.

Benefits of creating entry points

- Ministry leaders have contact with a larger pool of potential volunteers.
- Experienced volunteers are able to rub shoulders with and serve as mentors for new folks.
- Volunteers have a safe, low-stakes entry point.
- New volunteers know they will receive extra support from the ministry leaders.
- The ministry is shared among a larger pool of volunteers, taking pressure off the most committed volunteers.
- Training is kept to a minimum, allowing new volunteers to get a quick start.
- The church has an opportunity to observe volunteers in the area before placing them in roles of greater leadership.

- New volunteers have an opportunity to experience a low-stakes role before saying "yes" to higher-expectation roles.

"Fishing ponds"

It doesn't take someone who fishes to know that catching fish requires you to *go to the water*. The same could be said for recruiting volunteers. We have to meet them right where they live by creating "fishing ponds" where they can get started in service. Fishing ponds are an example of an entry-point program. They are designed from the ground up to give people a chance to dip their toes into your ministry area. We walk before we run. Development happens in degrees.

Example: A "fishing pond" for missions

FaithWork at The Church of the Resurrection provides a simple, ease-of-entry place to get started in missions. Twice a month, at 9:00 a.m. on Saturday, anyone from the church or community can show up in the narthex of the church. No reservations, no application, no requirements of spiritual maturity. Once they arrive, they are greeted at the door and presented with a list of service projects for the day, each lasting between two and five hours. Each project has a team leader who is standing under a sign with the project's name. After grabbing coffee and donuts, they visit with each project's team leader to find out more information about the day's activities. There are always a couple of projects advertised as being particularly appropriate for families with children. Some are on-site and some require travel to a local agency or another church. After a brief devotion and prayer, the teams are sent off for a morning of missions work.

The goal of FaithWork is, in part, to provide a way for people to do something meaningful with their Saturday morning. The aim is to have them return, and then return again. After they come back a few times, chances are they're ready for another step. One person's next step may be to lead a FaithWork project team. Someone else may become a weekly volunteer at one of the missions agencies they visited. At The Church of the Resurrection, we record the attendance of every FaithWork participant, and we frequently review our records for people who might be prepared to take their next step into deeper missional service. We gather feedback from team leaders asking if there was anyone who expressed desire to take another step of commitment.

POTENTIAL PITFALL

Note: Whenever you send volunteers to work directly with children and youth, observe your church's protection policies.

3. Spreading the word

Before tossing another announcement into the bulletin, let's take a step back. We should start with an understanding of your invitation message. What might cause someone to rearrange his or her personal schedule and say yes to volunteering? Start by answering the following questions. For help, you may want to poll current volunteers to get a handle on their answers.

MAKE TIME FOR THIS

- Why do current volunteers enjoy serving in this role?
- Why might others enjoy it?
- What is the best part of this role?
- What does this ministry do, ultimately?
- How can being involved in this ministry make a difference?
- What objections may someone raise to serving in this role? How might objections be overcome?

- Describe the people who are currently serving in this role. Are there trends in the gender, age, skills, motivations, etc. of the people who have said yes in the past?
- Could this role be a natural next step for someone who is already serving the church in a different capacity?

Your answers to the questions above will help guide your invitation strategy. For instance, one church was in need of five new nursery workers. The ministry leader started by describing her best volunteers. They tended to be empty nesters and post-retirement moms and dads who loved the church and attended very regularly. Since this church maintains an electronic database, a report was generated of men and women aged fifty to seventy who attended church more than 50 percent of the time. (A small church might be able to accomplish this with a downright low-tech method by simply using a membership directory and a highlighter.) Armed with this list, three dedicated current volunteers ordered pizza and met for one evening of phone calling. Before the pizza had gone cold, they had a full list of new volunteers ready for training.

Advertising your volunteer openings

▷ **Discover** that word of mouth is king. Why do new residents in your community decide to attend your church? Because they drove past the church building? They saw your ad in the newspaper? Or, were they invited to the church by a friend, coworker, or neighbor? Understanding what motivates response is important. At The Church of the Resurrection, each year we find that more than 90 percent of our new members decided to attend our church because someone they know personally invited them. Word of mouth is king. As a result, the foundation of our church's evangelism strategy has been built around supporting personal invitations. This dynamic is true for evangelism, and it works equally well for volunteerism. Motivated, enthusiastic volunteers are your key to a great invitation strategy.

▷ **Prepare** your "elevator commercial." It takes less than thirty seconds to ride an elevator. Thirty seconds is plenty of time to plant a seed in the mind of a potential volunteer. So, an elevator commercial is a compelling statement about the ministry that can be delivered in fewer than thirty seconds. It is brief, personal, and ends with a clear invitation.

Example: Food bank volunteer

"Each Monday I deliver food from our church's collection area to local shelters. It's amazing to see the impact of this ministry. Last week, I saw a single dad with three children eating a meal that was donated by a member of our church. I love doing this. The best part is knowing that someone is able to eat because the generosity of people in our church. You know, they always seem to need a few more drivers. Maybe we could serve together. Can I put you in touch with Joe, the guy who coordinates volunteers?"

Example: Usher

"I work as an usher once a month. It is a great place to serve not only because I get to greet our members but also because I get to be the first person to welcome our visitors. You usually never get to know their story, but recently there was a woman who came up to me after the service just to say thank you. She told me she hadn't been to church in years. I could see in her eyes how glad she was to be back. I'll never forget it. Hey, would

you be interested in joining the usher team? I know we have a few spots open for the first weekend of every month."

▷ **Have** volunteers prepare and practice their own elevator commercials at a volunteer meeting. Coach them to speak with enthusiasm, to share a personal story, and to give a clear "ask." Challenge them to share their commercial with at least three people in the next seven days.

▷ **Use** additional invitation ideas. If you find that word-of-mouth methods aren't adequate for filling volunteer needs, you may want chose from a variety of other methods of inviting volunteers.

▷ **Continue** different strategies for inviting volunteers.

- **Churchwide newsletter:** A great option for reaching the entire congregation. Make the most of the space by including stories and photos to increase the graphic appeal.

- **Ministry newsletters:** Make the most of ministry-specific newsletters, brochures, and hand-outs by providing information about current volunteer openings. Seek creative solutions to overcoming the readership limitations of your newsletter. Also, reserve space in your newsletter for a monthly volunteer highlight. Pick a volunteer the audience can relate to (not necessarily the most committed or experienced volunteer). Tell this volunteer's story, including how he or she got started and what obstacles had to be overcome to volunteer. In addition to being a source of encouragement for that particular volunteer, the story will help others picture themselves in ministry.

- **Bulletin announcement:** Typically one hundred plus or minus words with high visibility to all worshipers, including both members and visitors. Be sure to make the headline count. (The bulletin offers high visibility, yet generally yields a relatively low response rate unless supported from the pulpit.)

- **Pulpit announcements:** Verbal announcements are an excellent way to capture the story behind the volunteer need. The message has more to do with inspiration than information. Make certain to "strike while the iron is hot" by concluding with a simple next step that will allow potential volunteers to respond right away.

- **Broadcast e-mail:** Send a carefully worded teaser message in broadcast e-mail. The message should direct the congregation to discover more information by clicking a hyperlink to your ministry's web page. Once on your home page, they'll find content-rich pages and either a registration process or a link to e-mail you a response.

- **Targeted e-mail:** Generate a targeted e-mail list using defined parameters to reach your prime target. Consider which segments of the congregation you are most likely to reach (age, gender, previous involvement, worship frequency, zip code).

- **Bulletin tear-offs:** Some churches design their bulletins with a tear-off section that can be filled in and placed in the offering plate. This provides an instant response mechanism—and placing it in the offering plate supports the value of making a sacrificial gift of time.

- **Bulletin inserts:** A separate insert into the bulletin offers high visibility and an unrestricted layout for greater creativity. Consider seeking a volunteer with graphic design experience to assist with the layout.

- **Ministry fair:** Establish a churchwide, or a ministry-specific fair. Encourage ministry programs to creatively decorate their tables with posters and photographs. You may even consider award-ing a prize for the best booth. Volunteers who host the tables should be prepared to share their "elevator commercial" as many times as possible, with a sign-up sheet for instant response.

- **Calling blitz:** You can expect a strong response rate with such a personal appeal made by a cur-rent volunteer. Consider setting up a temporary phone bank in the church offices or in some-one's home using cell phones for the callers.

- **Preworship video scroll:** If your church utilizes video screen in the sanctuary, create a pre-worship slideshow of featured announcements. Otherwise, consider setting up a video projector or television in the narthex of the church with a loop of PowerPoint® slides or video interviews.

A donut shop has a sign that's difficult for me to drive past: "Hot, Fresh, Now." Whenever this sign is illuminated, it means that hot donuts are rolling out at that very moment—hot, fresh, and *now*. It gets me every time.

At The Church of the Resurrection, there was a time when we provided our new members with an exhaustive list of all the places where volunteers could potentially serve in the church. The list was expansive, with literally hundreds of places to serve. Impressive but ineffective. The trouble was, the list was always stale. Some of these volunteer opportuni-ties were only available during certain times of the year, such as fall kickoff. Other opportunities had already been ade-quately filled. The result was a poor connection rate for vol-unteers. We overhauled the strategy. Now we're "hot, fresh, *now*." We only list immediate opportunities where people could start serving right away—even tomorrow. In every case, a potential volunteer should be contacted within forty-eight hours of expressing interest.

The Connection Point

Think of the space near the main entrance to your sanctuary. Typically you'll find a dedicated place for newsletters, brochures, and information about the church. Many churches extend hospitality further by putting someone friendly in this space and calling it the Information Center or Welcome Station. The names we use to describe these spaces tend to define their ultimate purposes. *Information* and *Welcome* are both essential ingredients to the church.

Consider repurposing this space in your church. Turn it into a *"Connection Point."* Staff the Connection Point with one or more connection consultants selected because they are gifted and skilled at helping disconnected people become involved in places of growth, fellowship, and service. They'll continue to answer people's questions and they'll warmly greet visitors, but their true ambition is to match people with discipleship opportunities where they'll grow in their faith.

At the Connection Point, each consultant will be familiar with church ministries. Binders with current information should be available and consultants should be prepared to share just enough detail to allow someone to consider getting connected. They will know what Sunday school classes are studying, when the youth group meets, how to join the choir, and where in the church volunteers are needed this week. Most importantly, they'll know how to listen. A connection consultant will understand that newcomers can be intimidated by Christian lingo or may be uncomfortable making a long-term commitment.

The connection consultant will listen intently for an opportunity to connect the guest. At the conclusion of the conversation, the connection consultant will record the contact information and the contents of the conversation. Before sunset, the consultant will pass along all the important information to the ministry connector from that particular ministry area. This is a high-stakes baton hand-off. Time is of the essence, and the baton cannot be dropped—it represents the potential to change the world.

CHAPTER THREE

Connect

Perhaps the most engaging contest in the summer Olympics is the relay race. Not only are the racers sprinting at an unbelievable clip but also there is the added element of high drama—the baton pass. Every relay team knows the stakes are extremely high during the baton pass. They practice these two seconds again and again until the transfer of the baton from one athlete to another becomes a fluid, consistent movement.

When it works, it is magic. A successful hand-off keeps the team moving forward in stride. But a dropped baton will dash the team's hopes of a gold medal. If a baton hits the ground, it doesn't matter how fast the prior runners sprinted. The baton is critical.

Moving from invitation to connection in a ministry is a baton hand-off—and the stakes are high here too. Just as with the relay teams, if everyone handles the baton pass with precision, the team is on the way toward the finish line. And that's the goal.

So, an effective baton pass will go smoothly from invitation to the second component of a successful volunteer ministry program: to effectively *connect* volunteers into a ministry where they will be able to realize their ministry potential.

A Connection Strategy

A well-devised connection strategy will include three components: (1) developing position descriptions, (2) appointing a ministry connector, and (3) communicating shared expectations.

1. Developing position descriptions

It's one thing to put in time to bring home a paycheck; it is quite another to give your time away freely, without tangible benefit. As a volunteer, time isn't about money, but it is still valuable. Potential volunteers need to know that those in leadership roles take their time seriously. You have their name because they are contemplating an important time commitment, and they should have a clear description of what role they might be filling.

Volunteers also appreciate knowing that you have taken the effort to carefully consider the importance of their role. They want to see that you have clear expectations for their "job" and that they are taken seriously.

One way to do this is to create a position description (some churches prefer to call these "ministry descriptions") for every position you identified on your Needs Analysis Chart in the previous chapter.

- Position Title
- Ministry Impact
- Supervisor
- Primary Responsibilities
- Spiritual Gifts Needed/Desired
- Spiritual Maturity Necessary
- Additional Qualifications
- Availability Required
- Term of Commitment
- Training Requirements
- Additional Comments

2. Appointing a ministry connector

Each ministry in the church should have a designated *ministry connector.* The ministry connector acts as the bridge between the church and all the volunteer positions in a particular ministry area—matching, screening, and following up with volunteers during the connection process. Although you may want to assign this person responsibility for some of your *invite* tactics, this person's particular interest is in converting a potential volunteer into someone who is engaged in life-changing ministry according to his or her unique design.

The ministry connector stands at the figurative front door of the ministry, functioning as a one-stop volunteer human resources manager. And just like the HR department, this is usually not the person who manages the volunteers once they're on the job. A ministry connector is laser-focused on effectively connecting new volunteers according to their passions, abilities, and giftedness.

When choosing the ministry connector, be selective. Look for someone with the following traits:
- An enthusiastic champion and advocate of the ministry
- Loyal to the vision and leaders in the ministry
- Energized by people development
- A social networker—able to quickly bring people together
- Committed to thorough follow-through with every potential volunteer

Here's how it works. The ministry connector receives the names of potential volunteers from a variety of sources: personal referrals, the Connection Point, the pastor, new member follow-up, current volunteers, or the ministry director. The ministry connector initiates personal contact within forty-eight hours of receiving the name. Once contact is made, the ministry connector has three essential responsibilities: (1) matching, (2) screening, and (3) follow-up.

▷ **Matching.** With position descriptions in hand, the ministry connector has a face-to-face "interview" with every potential volunteer. The aim of the meeting is to ensure proper placement for the volunteer. The connector will ask questions and listen carefully for the interviewee's hopes and dreams. Together they will explore potential matches for the gifts, talents, and availability of the new volunteer.

If more than one potential match is identified, the ministry connector will extend an offer to help the new volunteer test-drive multiple options. For

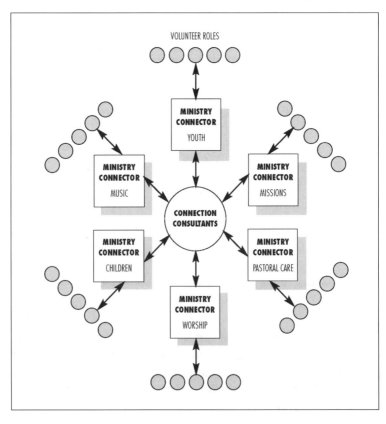

instance, a new children's ministry volunteer may be uncertain where in the ministry he or she should serve—whether as a hallway greeter, or as a nursery volunteer, or as a teacher in an elementary classroom. The ministry connector will arrange for the volunteer to "kick the tires" in each area before making the decision.

The ministry connector should also be aware of how spiritual gifts operate in Christian ministry. (See Rom. 12:4-8.) Several resources are available for evaluating giftedness. I recommend *Serving from the Heart* by Carol Cartmill and Yvonne Gentile (Nashville: Abingdon Press, 2003). This study can be used either individually or with a group and is written to help people discover God's design for their ministry.

POTENTIAL PITFALL

▷ **Screening.** Volunteer position descriptions should outline qualifications required for serving in the ministry. It should address the basic requirements of the position. Must I be a member of the church? Must I be a maturing Christian to serve in this capacity? Will there be a criminal background check? Does the church have certain expectations of my worship or small group participation? Can young teenagers serve in this role? Are there theological stances I must uphold to serve in this role? Sometimes firing a volunteer becomes absolutely necessary, but careful preventative screening is preferable every time (see page 56 about dismissing a volunteer). It is far better to have an awkward front-end conversation than to ignore the warning signs of an improper match. (Not everyone who expresses interest is placed in a particular volunteer position.) When a more formal screening process is in order, consider using an application. The application used during the committee nomination process at The Church of the Resurrection identifies the eight key elements of a successful match for serving on one of the committees. The committee overseeing nominations follows through with each applicant and also conducts reference checks as needed to ensure proper screening and matching. (See the Elected Leader Application at www.cor.org.)

➪ **Follow-up**. New volunteers are often anxious about their first day. It feels a bit like walking into a new high school or walking into the office on the first day of a new job. The ministry connector should ensure someone is prepared to greet the new volunteer and introduce him or her to the other volunteers. The new volunteer should be given an opportunity to job shadow until they become comfortable in the role.

As soon as possible following the initial experience, either the program leader or ministry connector should contact the volunteer to express appreciation and debrief the experience. The following questions may be a good starting place:

- How was your experience?
- Was it what you expected?
- Did you face any unforeseen obstacles?
- Did you sense that this is the proper role for you, or should we take a look at other positions of service within the church?
- Is there anything further we can do to assist you in this ministry?

The ministry connector will repeat the process with another formal check-in after the new volunteer hits the three-month mark to ensure proper placement. Again, this serves as an opportunity for an early course correction and communicates to the volunteer how much you value the gift of his or her time.

Note: Within small churches, these steps are particularly easy to overlook. Because you interact in such a close-knit community, it is easy to overlook the importance of formal check-ins. But keep in mind that most successful small businesses conduct annual employee reviews of their staff, just like the big companies. Even with just three or four employees, the principle behind the processes is important—perhaps even more so in a small setting.

3. Communicating shared expectations

If you are the identified leader of the volunteer ministry, it is your job to set the pace, define success, and establish a healthy volunteer culture. The following ideas may help you communicate common expectations for your ministry:

▷ **Establish** a Volunteer Bill of Rights. It should be posted in an office or workroom and will be presented for a new person's signature during the connection process. The Bill of Rights demonstrates a mutual commitment from every member of your team—staff and volunteers.

Volunteer And Staff Bill of Rights

1. Right to a suitable assignment match according to passion, personal style, spiritual maturity, gifting, life experiences, and availability.
2. Right to be treated as a fellow brother or sister in Christ.
3. Right to thorough initial and ongoing training.
4. Right to know about the ministry—including policies, programs, finances.
5. Right to sound guidance and direction by a more experienced person who is informed, caring, prayerful, patient, and thoughtful.
6. Right to a growth-oriented, gracious place to serve.
7. Right to be prepared for future service opportunities, whether inside or outside of this ministry area.
8. Right to have my opinions heard in the planning process.
9. Right to regular opportunities for service reflection with my supervisor.
10. Right to receive recognition and appreciation for my service.

⇨ **Develop** a Volunteer Leader Covenant. For leadership positions at the Church of the Resurrection, people sign a Volunteer Leader Covenant (see below). This covenant is required for volunteers serving as:

- elected church leaders, such as committee members,
- spiritual teachers or those designing educational curriculum,
- volunteer leaders involved in navigating the overall direction for a particular ministry area.

Volunteer Leader Covenant

Our lay leaders, along with our staff, fulfill the biblical roles of elders and deacons, shepherds and teachers. Throughout the New Testament, leaders are called to be examples to the rest of the church. As leaders, they are held to higher standards than other members. Paul sets forth lists of attributes of elders and deacons in his letters to the early church. Leaders should be "above reproach" and "not be puffed up with conceit" among other things. Peter, likewise, challenges leaders to be "examples to the flock" and to exercise leadership with a willing heart. Because leaders are held to a higher standard, James says, "not many of you should become teachers . . . for you know that we who teach will be judged with greater strictness."

As leaders, we set the tone and pace for the entire congregation. We model the Christian faith, the Christian life, and the attitude and heart of a Christian for our congregation. We shape the heart, character, and life of this Christian community. For this reason, it is vital that we walk the Christian walk. Spiritually healthy leaders will produce a spiritually healthy church. Likewise, leaders who fail to walk with Christ will have devastating consequences.

With this in mind, the following covenant was developed to guide our life together as leaders. We use these standards to hold ourselves accountable to pursuing the Christian life. And in so doing, we recognize that it is God's grace, which calls forth our faithful response, and it is God's grace, which brings such transformation in our lives.

I. THE GOAL OF THE CHRISTIAN LIFE: SANCTIFICATION

Jesus summarized the goal of the Christian life with two commandments: love the Lord our God with all your heart, soul, mind and strength; and love your neighbor as yourselves. John Wesley spoke of this goal as sanctification, Christian perfection, or holiness. In our Methodist tradition, three General Rules were designed to help Christians pursue this goal. As leaders we pursue these "rules" as we grow in faith and service together.

A. Avoid those things that are inconsistent with the life of faith, separate us from God, and bring harm to others, such as:

1. Self-destructive behavior (addictive behavior, poor self-care)
2. Moral compromise (sexual misconduct, greed, dishonesty)
3. Self-centeredness and pride
4. Malice (harboring resentment, acting in anger, backbiting)
5. Wasting of resources (the church's, or personal resources of time, talent, finance)

B. Do good of every possible sort, such as:

1. Live a life of love
2. Share our faith inside and outside of Resurrection
3. Care for our families
4. Build others up
5. Be engaged with those in need, both inside the church and out

C. Pursue growth in our spiritual lives, such as:

1. Attend worship each weekend, except when sick or out of town
2. Engage in close Christian friendships for spiritual growth and accountability in a small group
3. Serve God with our time and talents
4. Give in proportion to our income, with the tithe being the goal
5. Spend time in prayer and the personal study of scripture

II. THE HEART AND ATTITUDE OF A LEADER AT RESURRECTION

A. What is the heart and attitude of a Resurrection leader?

1. Humble (servanthood)
2. Positive
3. Joyful
4. Committed to Christ
5. Devoted to the purpose and vision of the Church of the Resurrection

B. How will Resurrection leaders live toward one another?

1. Demonstrating respect and grace
2. Accepting differences
3. Maintaining appropriate confidentiality
4. Publicly supporting other volunteer leaders, pastors, and staff members
5. Going directly to the individual whenever a problem arises

III. THE FAITH AND CHARACTER OF A UNITED METHODIST

The Church of the Resurrection is a United Methodist Church. We expect our leaders to honor our denominational heritage and to pursue ministry in keeping with our tradition.

United Methodists are people who seek to love and serve God with our head, our heart, and our hands. They are orthodox in faith, liberal in spirit, passionate, and deeply devoted to Christ, and desire to be wholly surrendered to God. They bring together both the evangelical and social gospel—inviting people to a life-transforming relationship with Jesus Christ, and then equipping and challenging them to live their faith in the public sphere, being engaged in the issues of our time and seeking to shape a world that looks more like the Kingdom of God. Methodists have been known as "reasonable enthusiasts"—valuing both a personal, passionate faith and one that is intellectually informed. Methodists are constantly looking to connect our faith to the world in meaningful, relevant ways. Methodists value spiritual disciplines and a "methodical" approach to growing in the faith. They strive for both personal holiness and social holiness.

United Methodists are not afraid to ask difficult questions, to take on tough subjects, and to admit that they do not always understand the answers. They are "people of the Book"—holding the Bible to be the inspired Word from God and encouraging people to read, study, and live by its words. "While we acknowledge the primacy of Scripture in theological reflection, our attempts to grasp its meaning always involve tradition, experience, and reason. Like Scripture, these may become creative vehicles of the Holy Spirit as they function within the Church."[1] Methodists also believe the Bible came to us through people who heard God's Word in the light of their own cultural and historical circumstances. And hence, they study the scriptures carefully, making use of scholarship and asking critical questions. And, as Methodists encounter theological differences amongst Christians, they bear in mind John Wesley's approach, "In essentials, unity; in nonessentials, liberty; and in all things, charity."[2]

Methodists are people who love God with all their heart, soul, mind, and strength, and love their neighbors. They pursue acts of piety toward God and acts of mercy toward others. They value passionate worship, relevant preaching, small groups to hold Christians accountable to one another, the need to address the social issues of our time, and the need to be people whose faith is firmly rooted in and built upon the scriptures. Methodists value the full participation of women and men, people of all races, classes and backgrounds in all facets of fellowship and leadership within the church and society.

This is our heritage, and it continues to shape The Church of the Resurrection in every area of our ministry.

1. *2004 Book of Discipline of the United Methodist Church,* ¶ 104.
2. Ibid., ¶ 102.

CHAPTER FOUR

Equip

THE GIFTS HE GAVE WERE THAT SOME WOULD BE APOSTLES, SOME PROPHETS, SOME EVANGELISTS, SOME PASTORS AND TEACHERS, TO EQUIP THE SAINTS FOR THE WORK OF MINISTRY, FOR BUILDING UP THE BODY OF CHRIST, UNTIL ALL OF US COME TO THE UNITY OF THE FAITH AND OF THE KNOWLEDGE OF THE SON OF GOD, TO MATURITY, TO THE MEASURE OF THE FULL STATURE OF CHRIST. WE MUST NO LONGER BE CHILDREN, TOSSED TO AND FRO AND BLOWN ABOUT BY EVERY WIND OF DOCTRINE, BY PEOPLE'S TRICKERY, BY THEIR CRAFTINESS IN DECEITFUL SCHEMING. BUT SPEAKING THE TRUTH IN LOVE, WE MUST GROW UP IN EVERY WAY INTO HIM WHO IS THE HEAD, INTO CHRIST, FROM WHOM THE WHOLE BODY, JOINED AND KNIT TOGETHER BY EVERY LIGAMENT WITH WHICH IT IS EQUIPPED, AS EACH PART IS WORKING PROPERLY, PROMOTES THE BODY'S GROWTH IN BUILDING ITSELF UP IN LOVE.
—EPHESIANS 4:11-16

Volunteers must be assured that they will be supported in their ministry. A well-designed equipping system will communicate the value you place on them and their development. The church has a stake in developing people, not because we want something from them, but because we want the best for them. Your equipping efforts will provide the essential support they need to take additional steps forward in their spiritual journey. Notice the thrust of the above scripture as Paul describes volunteerism in the early church. Ministry is about growth, maturity, and building up in love.

A few years back a ministry leader approached me with a complaint about his ministry. He was facing a significant challenge of finding leaders. "My church just doesn't do a good job of developing leaders," he shared. He went on to say that whenever he tried to move the ministry forward he couldn't; the church wasn't *giving* him enough leaders to accomplish his goals. There were plenty of *volunteers*, but not enough *leaders*. After reflecting on his dilemma, I returned to him with a question, "Whose job is it to develop your leaders?"

Four Keys to an Equipping System

No one has more responsibility for the development of leaders than you do. The discipleship and worship systems in your church are fundamentally important, but life-on-life ministry always carries the day in leadership development. Your church has no better development tool in its arsenal than putting people into hands-on Christian service in a healthy ministry. What does this look like? The *equipping* component of your volunteer ministry will provide fertile ground for spiritual growth. Four keys to an effective equipping system include: (1) apprenticing your volunteers, (2) utilizing a team structure, (3) training for the work, and (4) developing leaders.

1. Apprenticing your volunteers

In the Middle Ages, specialized artisans raised up future generations through an intentional apprenticeship process. Young apprentices would become understudies to master craftsmen, typically for a period of seven years. As apprentices, they

OOPS

When I was newly hired to oversee our youth ministry, I took a deep-dive into ministry with teenagers. I spent my time developing programs for them, attending events at their schools, writing birthday notes to them, and praying hard for their spiritual development. Of course, I interacted with adult volunteers, but I did so because I needed their help. Otherwise I wouldn't be able to do my ministry. An embarrassing number of years into my ministry, I hit the wall. I wised up and decided I shouldn't go it alone anymore. I began by creating a small group Bible study with our volunteers. I took volunteers with me to ministry conferences. I started sending birthday cards to them and delegating to the volunteers the birthday cards for teenagers. The focus of my leadership had shifted from solo, direct ministry with teenagers to overseeing a movement of adults in shared ministry with teenagers. The results were fantastic. More teenagers were involved in the ministry than ever before. I found I was able to accomplish more by focusing greater efforts on investing in volunteers.

served alongside a mentor who provided careful instruction and patient guidance. Those who developed their craft would later become journeymen within their guild, and a few would eventually become master craftsmen in their own right. And the cycle would repeat.

Jesus was the preeminent mentor—he turned a ragged group of social and spiritual misfits into world-changers. In fact, we are the legacy of this mentoring relationship. How did this happen? It took time with the master. He invested diligently in the lives of people who just couldn't quite seem to get their acts together. In fact, they bumbled the message and missed the point as they followed him. But they watched and observed the master teacher. And there was an atmosphere of trust and risk-taking. When they were sent on their first mission assignment, they were in way over their heads. But they had watched what Jesus did, and they had clear instructions. They gathered themselves together—and the world hasn't been the same since.

Apprentices should expect from their mentors:
- Encouragement
- Honesty
- Trust
- Grace
- Time
- Celebration
- Coaching

▷ **Think** investment. Mentoring is risky, costly business. It requires time, effort, and disciplined focus. As ministry leaders, we are tempted to deliver results quickly and efficiently. Just as soon as a program is finished, we move quickly to begin preparing for the next one. We're on a shoestring budget, and our plates are full with ambitious, urgent plans. This impatience leads to two common errors:

Error 1: Going Solo
We end up doing too much of the work ourselves. We become Lone Rangers. Going solo usually happens because we either didn't think we could trust someone else to do the task as well as we *thought* we could do it, or because we didn't budget enough time to walk someone else through the steps to succeed. **Solution:** Set aside a margin of time to slow down and invest in the development of others.

Error 2: Creating Sink or Swim Experiences

Occasionally we fall into the trap of unwittingly creating an environment of sink-or-swim. We churn through volunteers as we search for the one who comes ready-made for the task. We're looking for the one we don't have to develop. We seek a microwave solution to a Crock-Pot problem. **Solution:** Sometimes our ministries are blessed to acquire a "Stepford" volunteer. But, chances are, someone else already did the heavy lifting by investing time in this person. Someone mentored the volunteer to the point where he or she is now ready for this important assignment. Your job is to be on the lookout for people with untapped potential waiting to be developed. Ultimately, deep-impact ministry is found in *developing people, not acquiring them.*

Leaders with lasting impact—the ones who truly change the world—know their greatest impact in life is reproducing other people who have caught their vision and will carry it forward like a virus. If you want to radically change the world, invest in your volunteers.

▷ **Pray** first. What was Jesus' final activity prior to selecting his disciples, his closest ministry partners? Luke's Gospel contains the answer, "One of those days Jesus went out to a mountainside to pray, and spent the night praying to God. When morning came, he called his disciples to him and chose twelve of them, whom he also designated apostles" (Luke 6:12-13 [NIV]). Jesus committed himself to seeking God's will before he selected those in whom he would eventually entrust his ministry. Begin with prayer.

▷ **Demonstrate** learning. Mentors don't just teach, they show their apprentices how to learn. None of us has yet to arrive at the destination. In faith and in ministry, we learn together in mutual relationship. Being a great mentor has as much to do with asking the right questions as having the right answers. Together, you will be as iron sharpening iron. Even if you have vast ministry experience, you will undoubtedly learn from the volunteers as you do life together.

▷ **Structure** the process. If your ministry has fewer than eight volunteers, you may find that you are able to single-handedly mentor and develop the members of your team. But once you expand beyond a reasonable "span-of-care," you'll find your effectiveness diminishes. At this point you'll need to reinvent your role and entrust some of the apprenticeship of volunteers to other people. You have made an important transition; you have moved from shepherding to ranching. A rancher shepherds the shepherds. Ranching is accomplished through team-based ministry.

2. Utilizing a team structure

You are being stretched thin by the demands of ministry. If you have personal responsibility for too many details, programs, and people, you have a "span-of-care" issue. All healthy organizations, including corporations, sports teams, and churches, pay close attention to the span-of-care issue. They realize that whether you are a supervisor, a coach, or a manager, you have limits that cannot be ignored. At The Church of the Resurrection, for instance, we try to limit the number of people supervised by any one manager to six. If supervision is stretched further than this, there begins to be a breakdown in development and communication. When your ministry expands, you'll have to establish a team structure that grows with you.

When our church launched an ambitious new ministry, a satellite campus about twenty minutes away, we knew the need for volunteers and volunteer leadership would be immense. In order to succeed in this effort, we needed people to step forward—committed members and casual visitors alike.

We started by subdividing the overall ministry into five key smaller work areas (worship logistics, missions, children's ministry, youth ministry, and music ministry), and we invited a leader to serve as the point person for each area. Now we had six leaders, including the campus pastor. But the work was far too great to accomplish with six people. In order for the effort to reach its full potential, each of these five volunteer ministry leaders would build a team to come alongside him or her, particularly focused on an area of the program. With each member of each team contributing, we had multiplied the involvement to more than thirty people and had avoided the error of placing too much work at the feet of a few volunteers.

This is a model of reproducible teamwork. The pattern works at all levels up and down your church, from the highest level of leaders surrounding the senior pastor to the smallest tasks completed by occasional volunteers. And regardless of the size of your church, the principle of team will multiply the vision of the leader and ensure more persons are meaningfully involved in fulfilling the church's mission.

Team developmental sequence

Teams tend to cycle through various stages and there tends to be a fairly predictable rhythm to the life cycle of groups. Bruce Tuckman introduced a four-stage sequence of development that occurs in teams ("Developmental sequence in small groups," *Psychological Bulletin* 63 [1965]: 384-99).

> ▷ **Forming:** The team comes together and develops an understanding of the team's tasks and culture.

Though highly motivated, team members at this stage tend to act somewhat independently of one another. Strong leadership with clear vision is essential.

▷ **Storming:** Team members begin to voice their individual perspectives and challenge the social dynamics of the team. In healthy teams, this stage will be brief and beneficial. The group will emerge into the next stage with a stronger cohesion and sense of collective purpose. Leaders at this stage will listen carefully to concerns of individual members and move the group toward consensus.

▷ **Norming:** The group will share a stronger bond around agreed-upon values and behaviors. Collaboration is standard behavior and motivation is high. Individuals now act in greater concert and the leader's participation becomes more relational—functioning more as a collaborator than team leader.

▷ **Performing:** Not all teams make it to this stage. Those that do will find that team members now independently act on behalf of the entire team's goals. Very little supervision is required; the leader can become more indirect and now acts more as a participant. The group doesn't stay in this stage forever. Most teams continue to cycle through the storming and norming stages multiple times as they face internal or external challenges.

Later, Tuckman added a fifth stage of group life that he labeled **Adjourning**. In this fifth stage, we face the reality that a particular group may conclude its work or a team may have run the course of its effectiveness. This is natural. With volunteers, it is important the leader helps his or her team members to embrace the conclusion of their work together. Be careful as you consider the possibilities of how—even in the midst of closure—the work of the team can be affirmed, celebrated, and memorialized. Also, take care to guide each individual team member toward an appropriate next place of service.

3. Training for the work

In the past, training tended to come in two flavors: on-the-job and speaker on the stage in-service. Get creative! Consider a few of these options:

▷ **Attend** a conference together. Churches across the country are now offering ministry conferences at reasonable prices. Some conferences are held in your ministry area. Others, like The Church of the Resurrection's Leadership Institute, offer general sessions on leadership principles and practical breakout sessions on topics for every ministry area. If you travel to a conference, consider driving rather than flying. Not only will it reduce expenses but also the car time provides a perfect opportunity to prepare beforehand and debrief afterward.

▷ **Show** training videos. Many conferences and training events now offer videos of their sessions for purchase. Your entire team can experience great training at a fraction of the cost of traveling.

▷ **Start** a group blog or an online forum. Engage volunteers with content throughout the year by posting content on the web. You can link to trusted websites in your ministry area so volunteers can research on their own and develop their expertise in your ministry.

➪ **Visit** a local organization. Take your volunteers to a place where they'll catch another angle. Observe. Ask questions. Find out what ideas are beneath the surface. Use the opportunity to do some whiteboard thinking about your ministry area.

- If you want your program to become more welcoming to visitors, go to a restaurant known for outstanding hospitality. Ahead of time, set up an interview with the manager to find out what hospitality principles she can share.

- If you'd like to help your team become more innovative, visit an advertising firm. Gain from their expertise in understanding how to influence people.

- If your ministry is in decline, visit a business that was once in decline and turned itself around. Ask what worked, and what *didn't*.

- If you would like to sharpen your focus on intentional discipleship, visit a local fitness center and interview a panel of physical trainers to discover what they know about mentoring people through an intentional, comprehensive process of improving physical health. See how these principles might be instructive for you ministry team.

4. Developing leaders

Effective *training* and *leadership development* go hand-in-hand in an effective equipping system. The difference, however, is that *training* prepares a person to perform a task. *Leadership development* develops a person. Both are essential.

In general, organizations tend to do a better job of training than they do leadership development. This is because we are quick to ask for assistance whenever we don't know how to get something done. But we are less likely to seek guidance or coaching as we prepare our hearts and minds for effective ministry.

Your ministry has an opportunity to grow volunteer helpers into ministry leaders. Most people underestimate what God is capable of doing through them; volunteers have the potential to become more useful to God than they have imagined.

Volunteers in ministry will continually develop in their understanding of God's mission. They will learn about how God has crafted them for ministry. As servant-leaders, they will grow in faith as they give themselves away in the pattern of Jesus' ministry. Yet, even with a sense of humility, they will learn newfound confidence as they move boldly into new roles of life-giving ministry. They will discover strengths and gifts that they didn't know they had. Your volunteers will develop.

To aid the process of development, you will want to be intentional about creating a pathway for their development. Some ministries offer a leadership course or a series of courses to develop leaders (see pages 47-48). Other ministries opt for a less formal and more relational strategy. You may even choose to offer a churchwide leadership program or to band together with your colleagues from other local churches to collectively develop leaders for your specific ministry focus.

No matter what direction you choose, your design should foster growth in three areas: the *head*, the *heart*, and the *hands*.

The head represents our thinking. As we pursue growth in our minds we are expanding in our theological understanding of the Christian worldview. We are constant learners, studying from the pages of scripture and theological works. The goal is to move toward a sound understanding of faith—a Christian worldview. Bible study is the key component, balanced with other sources of sound teachings. Biblical underpinnings are specific to each area of ministry. By exploring the theology of ministry, you will help volunteers understand the nature and importance of the ministry to which God has called them.

The heart represents our relationships. We experience relationships in two directions—in our vertical relationship with God and our horizontal relationship with other people. The heart is the center of transformation; heady knowledge by itself falls short. Notice Jesus' statement that even the demons call him Lord (they had right knowledge, but wrong hearts). Volunteers are generous with their time, but they should also be growing in their spiritual disciplines (such as worship, prayer, and devotion) and in their relationships with other people. Take note that people rarely develop beyond the example of their leaders. Make certain you are modeling persistent growth in the spiritual habits you keep, including worship, study, giving, and prayer.

The hands represent Christian service. Your volunteers are already serving. They know how to translate knowledge (head) and transformation (heart) into a lifestyle of service to God and others. Your role is to stimulate their continued development as servant leaders who have an others-focused life. It is countercultural to have a life that places a higher priority on others rather than on ourselves. Paul encourages us this way, "Do nothing from selfish ambition or conceit, but in humility regard others as better than yourselves. Let each of you look not to your own interests, but to the interests of others" (Phil. 2:3-4). Look for opportunities to foster volunteers' growth as Christian servant-leaders.

CHAPTER FIVE

Sustain

Invite, Connect, Equip, Sustain. We place most of our focus on the front door, but successful ministries develop people for the long haul. Sustaining volunteers is an imperative. Practically speaking, you've invested incredible resources of your time, money, and energy in the invitation, orientation, and training and development of new volunteers. You've watched volunteers become an important part of the ministry. And they have become more and more effective over time. However, all this can dissipate if you don't sustain them in their ministry efforts.

Fact: When volunteers leave, they often won't tell you the honest-to-goodness reason *why* they left. They will tell the truth when they say, "I have a new commitment on Wednesday nights, so I just can't continue to volunteer." But the underlying reality is often that they didn't feel properly *sustained* in the ministry. When people feel this way they won't come right out and tell you. In fact, they may not even know it. But they have been inflicted with a low-grade virus of discontent. At this point they were still with you, but the virus was incubating. Then, once a competing opportunity came along, or they experienced conflict, or they encountered someone with a different theological opinion, they simply moved on.

Take note that even healthy ministries experience turnover. This is to be expected, and it can be a very good thing. New people bring fresh ideas and energy, and making room for new people to volunteer is an essential ingredient to connecting new members of your congregation. But, if you find that you are retaining less than 85 percent of your volunteers annually, your *sustain* plan may not be firing on all cylinders.

Sustain Plan

Let's take a look at three key components to a healthy **sustain** plan: (1) relationships, (2) reflection, and (3) recognition.

1. Relationships

Jesus spent three years of his short life living with his disciples. They weren't just coworkers. In fact, Jesus' primary agenda for changing the world was life-on-life ministry. As such, the disciples ate, drank, traveled, laughed, played, and cried together. They formed a bond of loyal friendship and mutual concern for one another.

MAKE TIME FOR THIS

One of the best things you can do with volunteers is to show them you enjoy their company. Set up times away from the program to simply build the bonds of relationship among your volunteers.

Suggestions for building relationships

▷ **Start** a weekly Bible study. If an extra evening isn't available, meet at a local restaurant for a sunrise study. Be sure to share the leadership of the lessons.

▷ **Join** in if one of your volunteers has a favorite hobby or recreation. Go fishing or bowling. Form a softball or volleyball team. Go antiquing together. Search for an activity that will allow the entire group to have fun while they celebrate the uniqueness of a volunteer coworker.

▷ **Dine** together. The dinner could rotate monthly to each person's house to increase the bond between volunteers. No meeting agenda, just recreation.

▷ **Incorporate** icebreakers and discussion starters in your volunteer meetings and training events. Be intentional about finding opportunities for sharing appropriate details about personal lives (describe your life when you were in third grade, share your idea of successful retirement, and so forth).

▷ **Retreat** together. Go to a local park or campground. Walk the trails, roast s'mores over a campfire. Share times of prayer and encouragement.

2. Reflection

Why do people have so many great ideas while they're in the shower? In the shower, we have no choice—we are forced to pause, to reflect. Could it be that our ministries suffer from a lack of reflection? Stop for a breather after a significant event, a lesson series, or the conclusion of a mission trip. Ask great questions. Reflection can either be done one-on-one with a volunteer or in a larger gathering with a team of volunteers. Ask big questions and make space for reflective answers. When an overly brief or insufficient answer is given, simply say, "Tell me more about that." You may want to use a few of these questions to get you started:

- What are your observations about what happened?
- What were your reactions to serving in this ministry?
- Were there any surprises?
- What worked? What didn't?
- What opportunity were we not prepared to meet?
- How can we better represent the ministry of the church?
- What would you say are the two most important conclusions you made about this ministry?

- As a result of your personal experience, what could you do differently?
- What should we all do differently next time?

▷ **Establish** annual evaluations. Employers use formal annual evaluations. Why? Performance improves when an organization invests itself in a process for the development of its employees. Similarly, volunteers should have a clear understanding of how they are doing in their role, what is expected of them in the coming year, and how they can improve. Thankfully, in ministry these evaluations can be less formal and more encouraging than employee reviews. Be certain to set an upbeat tone and let the appreciation and celebration flow freely. But don't miss the opportunity to annually discuss and evaluate. Your volunteers will appreciate knowing the depth of your desire to assist them along their development path. In addition to questions about their specific ministry, be sure to discuss the following:

- What has been your experience in ministry over the last year?
- What personal goals do you have for your ministry in the coming year?
- Are there any particular challenges you face in your ministry that I might be able to address?
- Do you sense that God is continuing to call you into this ministry?
- How can I do a better job of supporting you in your ministry?

After another personal affirmation of the volunteer, conclude the meeting with a prayer thanking God for this person and his or her family, and asking God's guidance for the coming year.

▷ **Conduct** exit interviews. Don't miss the opportunity to learn from the experiences of volunteers who are departing from your ministry. A formal exit interview will provide an avenue for gathering important feedback to improve the ministry. And it will also reestablish trust with those who may be leaving. You want people who leave to be great advocates; providing a pathway for their reflection and critique will make certain they leave knowing they have been heard. My preference is to have someone outside the ministry area conduct the exit interview. (Typically someone from our Committee on Lay Leadership conducts the exit interview and provides a written report of the conversation to the ministry leader.) The exit interview we have used at The Church of the Resurrection uses the following questions. You may want to personalize the questions for your particular setting:

- How was your experience while serving in this position?
- What did you like best about serving? What did you like least about serving?
- Describe the degree of support you received.
- Describe how well the ministry was organized.
- What were the particular challenges you faced when you first came on board?
- Did the ministry operate with openness, statesmanship, supportiveness, participation, and ability to set aside personal agendas?
- What changes would you recommend with regard to structure, length, format, or style of trainings and team meetings?
- How do you think the congregation perceives your ministry?
- To what extent were you able to grow personally and develop your leadership abilities? Describe

the training, education, or developmental experiences in which you participated.

- What additional learning opportunities would have been helpful?
- Do you feel that you made a significant contribution and that your time was well spent? What kind of feedback, if any, were you given along the way in this regard?
- What advice do you have for your successors?
- Have you determined where you will be serving next? (If you are uncertain, please speak with a consultant at the Connection Point.)

POTENTIAL PITFALL

⇨ **Realize** it may be necessary to release a volunteer. Since volunteers work for free, they can't be fired, right? In most cases they can, and in some rare cases it may be the healthiest thing you can do—both for the ministry *and* for the volunteer. If the ministry is being significantly hampered by a volunteer, consider releasing the volunteer. However, proceed with care and caution. Firing a volunteer is a measure of last resort, and unless there is a safety concern or a serious integrity issue, it should only be considered after formal meetings where clear expectations have been communicated. If established expectations have been repeatedly violated and personal coaching has proven insufficient, releasing the volunteer may be in order. Here are a few keys if you must face the situation:

- Meet face-to-face. If the conversation might become volatile, consider having a neutral third person present.
- Be straightforward and clear about what has led to the decision.
- Recognize the volunteer's positive gifts and abilities. If appropriate, offer options of volunteer roles that offer a better match.

- As a leader of volunteers, listen carefully for ways that you may have contributed to the situation. Remain open to the possibility that you have something to learn from the departing volunteer.
- Offer the exit interview discussed on page 55.
- Follow up with a personal note genuinely thanking the volunteer for time spent in service.

3. Recognition

Every volunteer deserves heartfelt appreciation for his or her ministry. The apostle Paul implores the church to "encourage one another and build up each other, as indeed you are doing" (1 Thess. 5:11). Don't let volunteers say that any ministry is a "thankless job." Make it a goal to see a smile break across their faces whenever people ask volunteers about their role.

> ⇨ **Establish** a *Recognition Champion* within particular ministry areas. This person's passion will be to find ways to be a blessing to volunteers. He or she will research other churches and organizations looking for great recognition ideas.

> ⇨ **Start** a churchwide *Recognition Team* to be an "extra set of hands" to help ministry areas show appreciation to volunteers. This team can develop ideas and themes for volunteer recognition parties.

> ⇨ **Host** a *Volunteer Recognition Weekend*. Publicly thank the volunteer team and simultaneously raise the value of volunteering within your congregation. Consider a churchwide annual emphasis on volunteers or a ministry fair (see chapter 2). Be sure to include personal stories of volunteers and testimonies of people whose lives are different because of volunteers. April is *Volunteer Appreciation Month*; consider making volunteerism an annual emphasis for your church.

▷ **Utilize** a *Pass on the Praise* card. Most churches have a place in the pews or chair pockets where offering envelopes and prayer request cards are found. Insert a card like the one shown here that will help you pass along personal stories of how volunteers are making a difference. When received, these cards are forwarded to the ministry area and the individual volunteer.

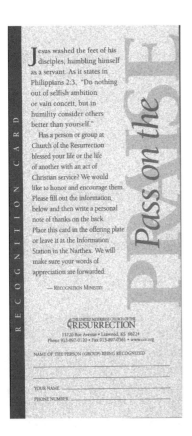

Top Twenty Easy Recognition Ideas

1. Provide permanent nametags to be worn by volunteers every time they come to church.

2. Solicit "thank you" handwritten notes from someone the volunteers serve. Distribute copies of the note to the volunteers along with a personal message from you reminding them how their ministry matters.

3. If your church has member nametags, distribute small stickers for your volunteers to affix to their nametags. The sticker should carry either your ministry's logo or a symbol of their volunteer service. This could also be a recruiting tool.

4. Provide certificates of recognition to volunteers for exceptional service.

5. You might try a little silly humor by creating false categories of recognition for each volunteer. Lean on ministry-insider humor and tell fun stories to go along with each volunteer's award.

6. Broadcast thank-you e-mails to the entire team after a big event or at the end of each year. Recognize each person's individual contribution to the program's overall success.

7. Recognize outstanding achievements in a special section of the ministry newsletter.

8. Send anniversary cards marking the annual date each volunteer started serving in the ministry.

9. Take the volunteer to lunch just to say thanks.

10. Distribute chocolate "hugs" and "kisses" to each volunteer.

11. Send each volunteer a personal birthday card thanking him or her for serving as a colleague in ministry.

12. Provide T-shirts with the ministry logo. This will increase common identity and serve as a helpful recruiting tool.

13. Display a large "Thank You, Volunteers" banner and have people sign it with notes of appreciation. Encourage pictures, quotes, and fun messages.

14. Photograph the entire volunteer team. Frame the photo and write a personal note of thanks on the back of each one.

15. Distribute candy bars with a note attached playing off the double meanings of their names. For example: You're worth *100 Grand.* You are one of the *Lifesavers. Kudos* for all you do!

16. Host a simple dinner for volunteers and their spouses or families. Be sure to express your deep appreciation for the volunteers' loved ones who make a hidden, but very significant, contribution to your ministry through the sacrifice of their time with the volunteer.

17. Send a friendly note whenever volunteers miss a week. Avoid creating guilt. Instead, use this as an opportunity to celebrate their time away while recognizing the importance of their work to the success of the program.

18. Create a "Wall of Fame" with individual pictures of each of the volunteers.

19. Clip magazine articles that recognize the value of the ministry. Distribute it to volunteers with a note of appreciation for joining together in the effort.

20. Include a listing of all the volunteer "staff" in the ministry's monthly newsletter.

Tips for Volunteers

You've done it. You have made yourself available as a volunteer in order to make a difference in other people's lives. It is a joy and a great privilege to serve in ministry.

Along with this privilege comes responsibility. Christian leaders are called to be an example for others. You will help set the tone and pace for your congregation. You will model the Christian faith, the Christian lifestyle, and the heart of what it means to be a Christian. And, you will shape the character and life of your church.

What kind of shape are you in? Wherever you are today, commit to moving forward. The direction of your life matters more than your arrival point. Along with volunteer service, step forward in your spiritual commitments, including: (1) consistent worship attendance; (2) participation in a small group for study, fellowship, and encouragement; (3) personal prayer and study of scripture; (4) financial generosity with the goal of tithing.

Remember, God provides others to serve alongside you. As a ministry team, you offer mutual support and encouragement to one another. The following tips will help volunteers make the most of their role.

Practical Tips for Volunteers:

▷ **Serve** according to your design. God's plans for your ministry are different than those of the person sitting next to you in the pews. You are unique and your gifts and graces for ministry are uniquely yours to express. Avoid the mistake of filling a need out of guilt, just because it was announced three consecutive weeks in church. Consider what issues or causes concern you most. Think about a time when you felt most alive as a volunteer. Take a spiritual gifts assessment to learn more about God's design for your personal ministry.

▷ **Memorize** the mission. Make certain you are crystal-clear about the ultimate aim of your ministry. Listen carefully to the vision of your senior pastor and the volunteer coordinator. Familiarize yourself with the biblical basis for your ministry. Know how to define success and understand the long-term impact of your efforts.

▷ **Demonstrate** loyalty. Seek to strengthen the leader-ship of those around you. The people you work with will not be perfect, including the church's pastor and staff. As a volunteer, you have the opportunity to bless, or to stir conflict. All too often, differences of opinion in churches are handled poorly. If you have a personal concern about someone in your ministry, your first step should be to humbly share your concern with that person. Together, seek res-olution and agree to support one another even in the absence of agreement.

▷ **Bring** others with you. Your greatest gift to the min-istry may be in multiplying yourself. Nothing can transform a ministry as quickly as a pumped-up vol-unteer bringing in new energy and resources. As an advocate for the ministry, your greatest legacy could be duplicating yourself. This simple effort could single-handedly take the ministry to a new level.

▷ **Pray**. In your car as you drive toward your volunteer responsibilities, get into the habit of praying for your service. You may want to pray something like this, "God, today I give you everything that I am. And I am grateful for the opportunity to serve you in this way. Please help me see you in the faces of the people I serve and, having encountered you, please help me leave as a different person. I surrender my life to you. Do with me as you will. Amen."

▷ **Serve** with joy. What a difference it makes to serve alongside someone who is perennially joyful! Serve with a happy heart. The apostle Paul was a great role model. He knew how to serve joyfully and find strength in the challenges of his ministry. In his times he faced enormous difficulties, such as prison, rejection, floggings, and being left for dead. Yet his letters reflect the profound joy he found in serving Christ. Paul says, "I have learned the secret of being well-fed and of going hungry, of having plenty and of being in need" (Phil. 4:12). Find joy in the ministry in which God has placed you.

▷ **Grow** your head, heart, *and* hands. Perhaps you said yes to a volunteer role to fill an important need in your church. Or maybe you said yes because you just aren't good at saying no. No matter how you landed in the role, you should consider it to be an important part of your spiritual development. Devote yourself to continued learning (head). Seek deeper relationships with God and others (heart). Serve generously according to your God-given design (hands). Many new volunteers face the challenge of adjusting to their new time commitments. But don't allow your spiritual life to suffer. Two important commitments will be worship attendance and participation in a small group Bible study for spiritual growth and accountability. Don't let these commitments slip as you volunteer your time.

▷ **Know** when to stop. Our lives have seasons. Perhaps your season to serve in a particular ministry has passed. That's okay. You may be experiencing a difficult time of transition, or stress, or illness and you sense that God is calling you into another season. You shouldn't "retire" from volunteering, but you may need to scale back or even step away for a time. Or, you may sense God calling you forward into your next ministry—one that is a better match for your unique gifts and experiences. The best volunteers know when it is time to step down or scale back.

Conclusion

Paul's words in Eph. 4:11-13 are instructive. Our work as leaders is to *prepare* or *equip* the people of the church for works of service; we are leaders in this effort to mobilize the people of our congregations into God-given service. Our role is to unleash the creativity, talent, and energy of our congregations and deploy the people of the church into life-giving ministry. This is what God has called us to be about.

When we get it right, lives are different. Our communities are transformed. Our churches are more effective. And our volunteers begin to tell us they are experiencing joy—the kind of joy that tells them they were "made for this." There is great pleasure in being caught up in this unbelievable adventure of ministry. We are participating in God's activity.

The tools found in this guide are a starting point. As you prepare to apply these principles, pause and ask God's help for ministry in your church. Pray for the current volunteers by name. Ask God to guide your steps as a leader and to empower you as you prepare God's people for works of service.